W9-BPK-745

BRAILLE ALPHABET

A	B	C	D	E	F	G	H	I
J	K	L	M	N	O	P	Q	R
S	T	U						Z

a	b			h	i
j	k			q	r
s	t			z	

COMMUNICATION
ALIKI

GREENWILLOW BOOKS, NEW YORK

MANY THANKS TO JUDITH FINESTONE

Watercolor paints, colored pencils, and a black pen were used for the full-color art. The text type is Symbol Medium; hand lettering was done by the artist. Copyright © 1993 by Aliki Brandenberg. All rights reserved. No part of this book may be reproduced or utilized in any form or by any means, electronic or mechanical, including photocopying, recording, or by any information storage and retrieval system, without permission in writing from the Publisher, Greenwillow Books, a division of William Morrow & Company, Inc., 1350 Avenue of the Americas, New York, NY 10019.   Printed in Hong Kong by South China Printing Company (1988) Ltd.   First Edition
1 2 3 4 5 6 7 8 9 10

Library of Congress Cataloging-in-Publication Data
Aliki.   Communication / by Aliki.   p.   cm.
Summary: Discusses the many different kinds of
communication and the functions they serve.
ISBN 0-688-10529-7 (trade). ISBN 0-688-11248-X (lib. bdg.)
1. Communication — Juvenile literature.   [1. Communication.]
I. Title.   P91.2.A44   1993   302.2 — dc20   91-48156   CIP   AC

COMMUNICATION

Communication is sharing knowledge.

It is telling news.

It is expressing feelings...

and being heard.

IT TAKES **TWO** TO COMMUNICATE

One to say it.

One to listen…

and respond.

You'll both be glad you did.

WE COMMUNICATE THROUGH LANGUAGE

We speak words.

We listen to words.

We write words.

We read words.

 We all need to express ourselves. Right.

BUT...

THERE ARE OTHER WAYS

Before early people learned to write, they communicated through pictures.

Even today, we use signs and symbols to communicate.

We communicate without words:

We touch, hug, and kiss. We applaud.

We stamp, push, pull, hit, and kick.

If we can't speak someone's language, we use body language.

Artists communicate through pictures, dancers through dance, musicians through music, ♪ writers and poets through words.

Other means of communication:

	letters	newspapers	books
magazines	telephone	codes	radio	television

LAUGHTER and CRYING are means of communication.

Whatever the reasons, people understand the meaning of laughter and crying.

Many people who are deaf communicate through sign language,
and they read lips.

People who are blind
read Braille with
their fingers.

ANIMALS COMMUNICATE, TOO

*I'm hungry!

*Welcome home!

*You're too close!

*This is fun!

BUT HUMAN BEINGS ARE THE GREAT COMMUNICATORS

And we all need someone to tell.

TELL ME

Go on, Jimmy.
Don't be uncommunicative!

But, Jimmy, you have to talk about it.

If you don't, do you know what can happen?

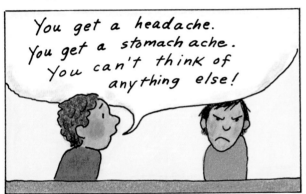

You get a headache. You get a stomach ache. You can't think of anything else!

Whatever it is grows and GROWS inside of you! It gets bigger than it is.

If you don't communicate, it causes pain and misery and suffering around you!

It causes misunderstanding and anger!

It causes pent-up emotions!

THAT'S HOW WARS START!

YOU ASKED FOR IT

— Abraham Lincoln.

SOME THINGS ARE EASY TO COMMUNICATE

Hi, Grandma! You should have seen what happened in school today. Our bunny escaped and nobody could find her anywhere...

Grandma must like to hear from Nikki, too.

SOME THINGS ARE HARD TO SAY

BUT IT'S A RELIEF WHEN YOU SAY THEM

FEELINGS are hard to communicate.

MY DIARY

Sometimes when a feeling is fresh,
it is hard to explain it to someone else.
So I communicate with myself.
I write it in my diary.
It helps me understand what is troubling me.

After that, I feel better.
Writing makes things clear.
It makes it easier to explain to someone else.
Sometimes just writing it down makes
the hurt go away.

But my diary is for fun and news, too —
and for remembering.

It's good practice
writing, too!

ARE YOU LISTENING?

FEEDBACK

Répondez, s'il vous plaît! *

Everybody needs some RSVP.

* That's French for feedback! Ha.

THANK YOU FOR TELLING ME

PEN PALS

THERE IS ALWAYS A WAY TO COMMUNICATE

Communicating is letting
someone else say something, too…

(even if you think you are fascinating).

Sometimes a book can communicate
your feelings to you.

IF YOU DON'T COMMUNICATE, YOU MAY NEVER KNOW

RACHEL LETS IT ALL HANG OUT

HAPPY BIRTHDAY

DID YOU HEAR?

Catherine's sister Caroline fell off her bike and sprained her wrist.

...Catherine and Caroline were going too fast and Caroline fell and broke her arm.

Someone pushed Catherine off her bike and she broke her arm and leg!

Bob's sisters Caroline and Catherine had a terrible accident!

...and poor Bob and his brother Matthew went to visit them in the hospital...

...and a car came along...

You know Matthew? Well, his brother and sisters are in the hospital...

...and all four bikes went flying in the air!

That's not the way I heard it.

If you're going to say it, at least get it right!

And now I'll sing you a song,
then I'll tell you a story, and a poem,
then I'll announce the latest news,
then I'll answer your questions...
then . . . hey, where are you?
Where is everybody?
I need to do it with somebody!

COMMUNICATION
*is the back and forth of telling
and listening and responding,
so you know you are not alone.*

UPPER CASE ALPHABET

A	B	C	D	E	F	G	H	I
J	K	L	M	N	O	P	Q	R
S	T	U	V	W	X	Y	Z	

SIGN LANGUAGE ALPHABET